A Divine Encounter
The Intercessor, the Prophet, and the King

Steve Harris

A Divine Encounter
The Intercessor, the Prophet, and the King

Steve Harris

Third Impression – December 2023
First Published in English in 2008 and in Mandarin in 2010

Published by Global Influencers
PO Box 308, Morningside QLD 4170, Australia
www.globalinfluencers.org

Copyright © 2008, 2021 by Steve Harris and Outpouring Ministries
All rights reserved

ISBN   978-0-6450343-6-3   (paperback)
ISBN   978-0-6450343-3-2   (eBook)

This book or parts thereof may not be reproduced in any form, stored in a retrieval system, or transmitted in any form by any means - electronic, mechanical, photocopy, recording, or otherwise - without prior written permission of the publisher, except as provided by Australian copyright law.

Scripture References

Unless otherwise indicated, all Scripture quotations are taken from the New King James Version®. Copyright © 1982 by Thomas Nelson. Used by permission. All rights reserved.

Scripture quotations marked (NIV) are taken from the Holy Bible, New International Version®, NIV®. Copyright © 1973, 1978, 1984, 2011 by Biblica, Inc.™ Used by permission of Zondervan. All rights reserved worldwide.
www.zondervan.com

Jeremiah 33:3
'Call unto Me, and I will answer you, and show you great and mighty things, which you do not know.'

Since the age of 10, God has from time to time, chosen to take me up into the Heavenly realms, and to open my eyes to see and my ears to hear some of the amazing and glorious things that are taking place there.

Scripture indicates that as we move further into the Last Days, these types of experiences will become much more common for all who believe in Jesus Christ (**Joel 2 : 28-29**).

Our God is supernatural and while earthly things will eventually pass away (**Luke 21 : 33**), He is the same yesterday, today, and forever (**Hebrews 13 : 8**). The realms of Glory are real, and God is always willing and able to take us up so that we can see, learn, and be changed from glory to glory (**John 1 : 51, 2 Corinthians 3:18, Revelation 4 : 1**).

What follows is the account of an amazing
supernatural encounter that took place
a few years ago during the 7th watch
(midnight to 3am).

It was an experience that was just as real
as the air that we breathe and the food
that we eat, except that it did not
take place in the earthly realm.

Time does not behave in the spiritual realms
as it does in the earthly realm.

When the experience ended,
although the clock on the wall said 3 a.m.,
from inside the Divine encounter
time seemed to be without beginning or ending.

My earnest prayer is that, as you read,
you will be inspired and challenged,
and become hungrier to go much deeper
into the realms of the Spirit as you pray
and seek the face of Almighty God
during your own devotional times.

A Divine Encounter
The Intercessor, the Prophet, and the King

In the middle of a time of deep devotions :

I was taken in the Spirit to a location on top of a hillside in Israel. The landscape resembled the hill country that is adjacent to Jerusalem.

There were hills and mountains all around. It was very windy; but the wind was not physical. It was the wind of the Holy Spirit.

I was not aware of my body at all, only of my spirit.

I could hear and feel that the wind of the Spirit was blowing strongly from many directions simultaneously; and I was also very aware of the very strong, thick, weighty Presence of God.

His Presence permeated the air, the hilltops, and all of the surrounding area.

Suddenly, from behind me and to my left, a sound began. It was unlike any heavenly or earthly sound that I had ever heard before in my life.

Somehow, the sound simultaneously tore at my heart and lifted my spirit.

It started softly and grew in volume and intensity until it permeated every part of me just as the Presence of God already was.

The sound lasted for a very long time. It was having a physical effect on the earth beneath and on the realms above – and as the sound continued, the atmosphere and the earth were changed by it.

The earth began to groan, and the wind changed direction as the sound continued.

My spirit was deeply affected by all of this.

The experience was so awe-inspiring, I did not want to do or think anything at all that could possibly interrupt the breathtakingly awesome and beautiful Divine flow.

I was given understanding by the Spirit of God, that this sound that I was hearing, this beautiful, strange and unearthly sound, *that was literally changing heaven and earth,* was the sound of a man praying, groaning, crying out to God from the very depths of his being, with literally *all* that was within him.

I was filled with awe because I had never in all my life heard a prayer that resembled anything like this.

I listened intently and tried to understand the sounds, the meaning, and the depth of this prayer.

The Holy Spirit wind, the prayer, the sound, and the deep groaning continued for what seemed like about one hour.

Then, as suddenly as it had started, it stopped. The echo of the sound filled the air for quite some time after the actual prayer had stopped. It was awe inspiring to behold this outpouring of pure spiritual sound echoing throughout the heavens above and the earth below.

After a period of silence, again not wanting to disturb the flow or intrude at all into this holy and sacred experience, I felt an urge to raise my head. And so, very carefully and quietly, I looked up.

And I saw, standing in front of me at a slight distance, and slightly to the right (opposite to the direction that the prayers had come from) a very large, muscular man. His head was bowed and his hands were folded.

He had been listening intently to the prayer of the other man. He was dressed in tattered clothing, with a breastplate of studded leather, of the type that is worn into battle.

His clothes were torn and his skin was covered in sweat, dirt, and blood. He had leather sandals and was dressed in soldier's gear. His hair was long and matted and he had a beard. From his appearance, he looked as though he had been on the front line of many battles and wars.

He lifted his face and I realized then that I was in the presence of a mighty king.

His bearing was royal, and his anointing was strong. His eyes were brilliant and kingly, yet also filled with sadness and pain. He looked long and hard in the direction that the prayer had come from.

Behind him I noticed three sets of rough sawn pieces of timber. There were three sets of horizontal and vertical pieces that had the appearance of both post and lintel doorways, and crosses.

The king cupped his hands in front of him; and as he did so, the prayers of the other man were gathered to him, by the Spirit of the LORD, into his hands. The reverberating sounds literally were swept into his cupped hands.

Then, he lifted his hands towards Heaven and as he did, he opened his mouth and began to sing (although I could not hear the song). He was worshipping and giving praise to God with his entire being. As he worshipped, his face became radiant with the Glory of the LORD.

As he lifted his hands, the prayers that had been gathered into his hands by the Spirit took on a physical appearance so that they resembled strips of white cloths or scrolls.

As the scrolls formed, they were growing in length and being pulled upwards by the wind of the Spirit.

These scrolls had the entire text of the first man's prayers written upon them, and they were being combined with the glorious worship of the warrior king.

I now suddenly found myself in the midst of a powerful whirlwind that seemed to emanate from the hands of the king. This whirlwind of the Spirit was carrying the prayers and the worship upwards and out of sight of the earth.

The whirlwind was being created by the Spirit of the LORD. The whirlwind created a swirling hole - a Heavenly portal - through the Glory Cloud of God that was directly overhead. The Throne of God was directly above the cloud.

It was not directly visible, but the Presence of the LORD was overwhelmingly strong, awesome, and beautiful; and the lightning and thunder of the Throne Room could be seen and felt through the Heavenly portal that was penetrating the cloud of Glory.

I heard the words "whirlwind of Elijah" in the Spirit. I was trembling. This was so holy.

From my vantage point, I could see that the prayers, represented by the cloths / scrolls, were being taken up by this whirlwind directly to the Throne of God.

It was amazing and awe-inspiring to behold. The prayers, and the worship, spoken and sung here on the earth, were, in the next instant, translated by the Spirit of God through the whirlwind of the heavenly portal, until almost instantly, they were right before the Glorious Throne of Almighty God.

Eventually I was brought back down to the same hillside in Israel, surrounded by hills and mountains.

There was a long period of silence and relative stillness. In my spirit, I was trying to take in the magnitude and significance of everything that I had witnessed so far. I did not want to move. The Presence of the LORD was so strong, and I felt so unworthy to be in this holy, sacred place.

After a period of grace and reflection that I was given, I began to understand that it was *my turn* to pray.

After everything that I had just witnessed, I was awestruck. The last thing that I wanted to do was speak or pray but the Spirit of God urged me on. And so, I opened my heart, and my mouth, in faith.

And as I did so, the sounds that came forth were very similar to the ones that I had experienced earlier coming from the other man.

The prayers and groans and sounds that came out of me, had an effect on the earth and the heavens, that was very similar to the effect of the first man's prayers.

My prayers and deep groanings lasted for about the same time as the first man's prayers; and when the sound of the Spirit had stopped coming out of me, it also echoed and reverberated through the earth and through the air, changing them and transforming them.

When I was done, there was a period of silence.

I realized that the king had been listening just as intently to my prayers as he had to the first man's.

I watched in amazement as by the Spirit of God, my prayers were gathered into the cupped hands of the king.

I watched as he lifted his cupped hands in worship, and this time as he opened his mouth, I heard him sing the most beautiful song of worship to God.

I was awestruck by the beauty of the king's heartfelt worship. It was simply unlike anything I had ever heard on the earth. There are no words to describe this song.

As this battle hardened warrior king offered the prayers up to Heaven, accompanied by his amazing worship, once again the whirlwind of the Spirit took the scrolls (my prayers) and the worship of the warrior king immediately up to the Throne of God, into the Glorious presence of the LORD, into the lightning and thunder, and before the glorious throne of the King of Kings.

Then, it was my turn to gather the prayers of the others. I stood in the place where the king had been standing. The others prayed.

I gathered their prayers by the Spirit of the LORD into my cupped hands; I lifted my hands and offered up their prayers, mixed with my worship; and the prayers turned into scrolls were immediately taken up in the rushing whirlwind straight to Heaven, to the Throne of Almighty God.

After all of this was completed, I found myself back on the same hillside, overawed and completely humbled by all that had taken place.

God was there, silent, and waiting.

After a long time of just waiting in His intimate Presence I quietly asked Him, "God, who was that who prayed?"

After a long pause, He answered me. He spoke and told me, "That man who prayed was the same one who wrote down the words of the Book of Lamentations.

I then lifted my eyes and looked once again at the warrior king. It was not necessary to ask God who it was; because it was clear that I had been in the company of none other than King David himself – David, the warrior king, the sweet Psalmist of Israel.

The prophet Jeremiah was the one who wrote down the Book of Lamentations.

And the spirit of Elijah the prophet was there in the whirlwind.

The thing about Jeremiah and David that was the most striking to me during this experience was the extent to which they were "poured out vessels."

Jeremiah was a broken and pure vessel that the Holy Spirit could use without reservation. That is why his prayers were so powerful — pure Spirit flowing through his surrendered heart. King David also appeared as a broken, pure, empty, poured out vessel that the LORD could truly use. The glory and beauty of the Spirit song flowing through the heart of the warrior king is something that I'll never forget.

Behind King David there were three sets of roughly sawn pieces of timber. There were three sets of horizontal and vertical pieces that had the appearance of both post and lintel doorways, and crosses.

I

believe that they represented both the complete surrender of one's life, regardless of the suffering, circumstances, or consequences, in order to serve God completely; and the three doorways of intercession, worship and prophecy that can only be truly opened by one who has willingly shared in the sufferings of Christ at least in some measure.

The only way through to experience the Glory of God in this life is if there is a surrendered willingness to also share in His sufferings – this is the way of the Cross.

If we are willing to embrace the Cross - if we are willing to truly walk with our LORD Jesus Christ, wherever He may lead, then He will open up the realms of Glory to us.

It is clear from this powerful divine encounter that true, Spirit-inspired and Spirit-led intercession and worship can literally move and transform heaven and earth if the vessels through which they flow have been truly shaped by the LORD and have no desire other than to be used by Him.

It is also true to say that GOD desires deeply to raise up many Jeremiahs (true intercessors), Davids (true worshippers) and Elijahs (true prophets) in our day, and in our time.

He is looking for vessels who are willing to be utterly broken and shaped by His hand.

He is looking, once again, for men and women who are willing to pay the price.

Selah, and Amen.

A Divine Encounter
The Intercessor, the Prophet, and the King

Biblical References

Some of the prayers of Jeremiah which are recorded in the Book of Lamentations

Jeremiah carried the burden of an entire nation and his life was consumed by God's passion for a people who had strayed far from Him.

Lamentations 3 : 22-24
Through the LORD's mercies we are not consumed, because His compassions fail not.

They are new every morning;
Great is Your faithfulness.

"The LORD is my portion," says my soul,
"Therefore I hope in Him!"

Lamentations 3 : 40-41
Let us search out and examine our ways,
And turn back to the LORD;
Let us lift our hearts and hands
To God in Heaven.

Lamentations 3 : 49-50
My eyes flow and do not cease,
without interruption,
Till the LORD from Heaven
looks down and sees.

Intercession

Romans 8 : 26-27
Likewise the Spirit also helps in our weaknesses.
For we do not know what we should pray for
as we ought, but the Spirit Himself makes
intercession for us with groanings which
cannot be uttered.

Now He who searches the hearts
knows what the mind of the Spirit is,
because He makes intercession for the saints
according to the will of God.

2 Chronicles 7 : 14-15

"... if My people who are called
by My name will humble themselves,
and pray and seek My face,
and turn from their wicked ways,
then I will hear from heaven,
and will forgive their sin
and heal their land.

Now My eyes will be open
and My ears attentive
to prayer made in this place."

Jeremiah 29 : 13

And you will seek Me and find Me,
when you search for Me with all your heart.

1 Peter 3 : 12

"For the eyes of the Lord
are on the righteous,
And His ears are open
to their prayers;
But the face of the Lord
is against those who do evil."

Scrolls

Psalm 40 : 7-8 (NIV)
Then I said, "Here I am, I have come
- it is written about me in the scroll.
I desire to do your will, O my God;
your law is within my heart."

Psalm 56 : 8 (NIV)
Record my lament;
list my tears on your scroll
 - are they not in your record?

A Scroll of Remembrance

Malachi 3 : 16-18 (NIV)
Then those who feared the LORD talked with each other, and the LORD listened and heard. A scroll of remembrance was written in His Presence concerning those who feared the LORD and honored his name.

"They will be Mine," says the LORD Almighty, "in the day when I make up My treasured possession. I will spare them, just as in compassion a man spares his son who serves him. And you will again see the distinction between the righteous and the wicked, between those who serve God and those who do not."

The effects of our prayers

Matthew 18 : 19-20
"Again I (Jesus) say to you that if two of you
agree on earth concerning anything that they ask,
it will be done for them by My Father in heaven.
For where two or three are gathered together in
My Name, I am there in the midst of them."

James 5 : 16-18
The effective, fervent prayer
of a righteous man avails much.
Elijah was a man with a nature like ours,
and he prayed earnestly that it would not rain;
and it did not rain on the land
for three years and six months.

And he prayed again,
and the heaven gave rain,
and the earth produced its fruit.

Acts 4 : 29-31
"Now, Lord, look on their threats, and grant
to Your servants that with all boldness they
may speak Your word, by stretching out
Your hand to heal, and that signs and wonders
may be done through the Name
of Your holy Servant Jesus."

And when they had prayed, the place where they
were assembled together was shaken; and they
were all filled with the Holy Spirit, and they
spoke the word of God with boldness.

Worship

2 Chronicles 5 : 11-14

And it came to pass when the priests came out of the Most Holy Place (for all the priests who were present had sanctified themselves, without keeping to their divisions), and the Levites who were the singers, all those of Asaph and Heman and Jeduthun, with their sons and their brethren, stood at the east end of the altar, clothed in white linen, having cymbals, stringed instruments and harps, and with them one hundred and twenty priests sounding with trumpets - indeed it came to pass, when the trumpeters and singers were as one, to make one sound to be heard in praising and thanking the Lord, and when they lifted up their voice with the trumpets and cymbals and instruments of music, and praised the Lord, saying:

"For He is good, for His mercy endures forever," that the house, the house of the Lord, was filled with a cloud, so that the priests could not continue ministering because of the cloud; for the glory of the Lord filled the house of God.

Psalms 42 : 7-8
Deep calls unto deep
at the noise of Your waterfalls;

All Your waves and billows
have gone over me.
The Lord will command
His lovingkindness in the daytime,

And in the night His song shall be with me
- a prayer to the God of my life.

Psalms 19 : 1-4
The Perfect Revelation of the Lord.
To the Chief Musician. A Psalm of David.

The heavens declare the glory of God;
And the firmament shows His handiwork.
Day unto day utters speech,
And night unto night reveals knowledge.

There is no speech nor language
Where their voice is not heard.
Their line has gone out through all the earth,
And their words to the end of the world.

Psalms 84 : 1-2
The Blessedness of Dwelling
in the House of God.
To the Chief Musician.
On an instrument of Gath.
A Psalm of the sons of Korah.

How lovely is Your tabernacle,
O Lord of hosts!
My soul longs, yes, even faints
For the courts of the Lord;
My heart and my flesh
cry out for the living God.

Psalms 89:15-16
Blessed *are* the people
who know the joyful sound!
They walk, O Lord,
in the light of Your countenance.

In Your name they rejoice all day long,
And in Your righteousness they are exalted.

Revelation 5 : 11-14
Then I looked, and I heard the voice
of many angels around the throne,
the living creatures, and the elders;
and the number of them was
 ten thousand times ten thousand,
and thousands of thousands,
saying with a loud voice:
"Worthy is the Lamb who was slain
To receive power and riches and wisdom,
And strength and honor and glory and blessing!"

And every creature which is in heaven
and on the earth and under the earth
and such as are in the sea,
and all that are in them, I heard saying:

"Blessing and honor and glory and power
Be to Him who sits on the throne,
And to the Lamb, forever and ever!"

Then the four living creatures said, "Amen!"
And the twenty-four elders fell down and
worshiped Him who lives forever and ever.

King David the Warrior

1 & 2 Samuel (many references)

King David the Worshipper

2 Samuel 23 : 1-4
Thus says David the son of Jesse;
Thus says the man raised up on high,
The anointed of the God of Jacob,
And the sweet psalmist of Israel:

"The Spirit of the Lord spoke by me,
And His word was on my tongue."

King David the Psalmist

The Book of Psalms
(most of the poems, songs, and prayers
contained within the Books of Psalms
were written by King David)

Whirlwind

2 Kings 2 : 11
Then it happened, as they continued on
and talked, that suddenly a chariot of fire
appeared with horses of fire, and separated
the two of them; and Elijah went up
by a whirlwind into heaven.

Psalms 77 : 18
The voice of Your thunder
was in the whirlwind;

The lightnings lit up the world;
The earth trembled and shook.

Ezekiel 1 : 4
Then I looked, and behold, a whirlwind
was coming out of the north, a great cloud
with raging fire engulfing itself;
and brightness was all around it
and radiating out of its midst
like the color of amber,
out of the midst of the fire.

The Throne Room of Heaven

Revelation 4 : 1-5
After these things I looked, and behold,
a door standing open in heaven.
And the first voice which I heard was like
a trumpet speaking with me, saying,
"Come up here, and I will show you things
which must take place after this."

Immediately I was in the Spirit; and behold,
a throne set in heaven, and One sat on the throne.
And He who sat there was like a jasper and
a sardius stone in appearance; and there was
a rainbow around the throne, in appearance like
an emerald.

Around the throne were twenty-four thrones,
and on the thrones I saw twenty-four elders
sitting, clothed in white robes; and they had
crowns of gold on their heads. And from
the throne proceeded lightnings, thunderings,
and voices. Seven lamps of fire were
burning before the throne, which are
the seven Spirits of God.

INVITATION TO MAKE YOUR PEACE WITH GOD

Dear Friend, it's possible that you have read this booklet because someone who loves you very much has given it to you. It's also possible that you have read this far, without knowing Jesus Christ as LORD, or without understanding that you need to make your peace with God.

If that is you, please read on, because I would like to explain to you how easy it is, and how wonderful it is, to receive Jesus Christ into your heart and into your life. He wants to give you the free gift of eternal life, and it is as easy as sincerely believing in Him and sincerely receiving Him.

Step 1 - Understand that God has a plan for your life – and it's a good plan

His plan for you involves the free gift of true love, peace, joy, and abundant and eternal life.

Jeremiah 29:11 (NIV)
"For I know the plans I have for you," declares the LORD, "plans to prosper you and not to harm you, plans to give you hope and a future".

Romans 5:1 (NIV)
*We have peace with God
through our LORD Jesus Christ.*

John 3:16 (NIV)
*For God so loved the world
that He gave His only begotten Son,
that whoever believes in Him
should not perish but have everlasting life.*

John 10:10 (NIV)
*I (Jesus) have come that they may have life,
and that they may have it more abundantly.*

Step 2 - Understand that your life choices have separated you from God

God created us in His own image, and He gave each of us the gift of free will and free choice.

Unfortunately, most of us did not understand or appreciate this gift, and the choices that we have made have taken us far from the path of divine destiny and eternal love that was meant just for us.

This has resulted in separation from God and from His wonderful plan for our life.

The Bible says in **Romans 3:23** :-
For all have sinned and fall short of the glory of God.

And in **Romans 6:23 (NIV)** we read :-
For the wages of sin is death, but the gift of God is eternal life in Christ Jesus our LORD.

Proverbs 14:12 (NIV) says :-
"There is a way that seems right to a man, but in the end it leads to death."

Isaiah 59:2 (NIV)
But your iniquities have separated you from your God; your sins have hidden his face from you, so that he will not hear.

Step 3 - Understand that God has made a Way back to Himself through the Cross of Calvary

God knew that many, in ignorance of the truth, would walk away from Him. And so, He provided a way for us to return to Him. He sent His one and only beloved Son, Jesus Christ to die on the Cross as a sacrifice for our sins and wrong doing.

Because of His sacrifice, we can have peace with God, if we are willing to repent (change our way of thinking about God, ourselves, and others) and to receive His free gift of salvation.

Not only did Jesus die in our place and pay the penalty for our sins, but He defeated the power of death and rose from the grave.

He now personally invites each of us to follow Him into eternal life and eternal glory.

Romans 5:8 (NIV)
But God demonstrates his own love for us in this:
While we were still sinners, Christ died for us.

Colossians 1:19-22 (NIV)
For God was pleased ... through Him (Jesus)
to reconcile to Himself all things, whether things on
earth or things in heaven, by making peace through his
blood, shed on the cross.

Once you were alienated from God and were enemies
in your minds because of your evil behavior.

But now he has reconciled you by Christ's physical body
through death to present you holy in his sight,
without blemish and free from accusation.

1 Timothy 2:5 (NIV)
For there is one God and one mediator
between God and men, the man Jesus Christ.

Step 4 - Trust and believe God, and make your own decision to receive Christ into your heart, TODAY.

If you have read this far, it is because God is speaking directly to you, and He is calling you to take your rightful place as a member of His eternal family.

This is the most important decision of your life, and it is a decision that will activate God's gift of eternal life within you as soon as you make it. The best time to make this decision is – today.

Hebrews 4:7 (NIV)
Today, if you hear his voice, do not harden your hearts.

Romans 10:9 (NIV)
*If you confess with your mouth, 'Jesus is LORD,'
and believe in your heart that God raised Him
from the dead, you will be saved.*

John 1:12 (NIV)
*Yet to all who received him,
to those who believed in his name,
He gave the right to become children of God.*

Step 5 – Pray – Talk to God – Tell Him that you have decided to come back to Him

Prayer is talking to God. Your first prayer is your first conversation with your Creator, and through it, if your heart is sincere, He is about to give you the gift of eternal life. All you have to do is ask Him for it. Prayer simply means "talking with God." You can speak to Him through prayer in the same way that you speak to a person.

Please pray the following prayer, with a sincere heart. There is no need to feel shy or hesitant. Your Creator God has been waiting and longing for you to have this exact conversation with Him, since the beginning of time.

"LORD Jesus, I know that I am a sinner and that I need Your forgiveness. Today I choose to repent - to change my way of thinking about You, myself, and others.

I believe that You died for my sins. I want to turn from my sins and live a life that is pleasing to you. I want to live according to Your plan for my life, and I need Your help to do that.

I now invite You to come into my heart and life. I want to trust and follow You as LORD and Savior. I ask and pray this in Jesus' Name. Amen."

If you prayed this prayer sincerely, the Bible assures you (in **Romans 10:13 (NIV)**) that:-

*Everyone who calls on the
Name of the LORD will be saved.*

And in **Ephesians 2:8-9 (NIV)**
we have this assurance :-

*For it is by grace you have been saved,
through faith - and this not from yourselves,
it is the gift of God - not by works,
so that no one can boast.*

Congratulations, and welcome to the family of God! Your life will never be the same again.

The Bible says that angels are rejoicing right now because of your decision.

Luke 15:10
"In the same way, I tell you, there is rejoicing in the presence of the angels of God over one sinner who repents."

Now, it's essential that you continue to walk in the pathway of your new life as a member of the family of God. The next page contains some helpful advice to help you to do that.

How to Walk With God

Here are some important steps that will help you to grow and become a strong Christian :-

1) Obtain a Bible and read it every day;

2) Seek out the friendship and fellowship of other Christians who are walking strongly with God;

3) Talk to God in prayer every day;

4) Tell others about your decision to follow Jesus;

5) Ask the person who gave you this booklet, or other Christians that you may know, if they can help you to find a good local church where you can spend time with committed Christians, who can help you to grow stronger in your faith.

6) Find out about water baptism
   (God will seal you as His own);

7) Find out about the Baptism of the Holy Spirit
   (God will fill you with His divine power to live a powerful, supernatural life). God bless you !

About the Author

Apostle Steve Harris has walked with Jesus since 1987. He has been blessed to worship with ministers such as Ron Kenoly and Pastor Benny Hinn.

He has taught the Word of God and preached the Gospel in many nations of the world, with salvation, healing, and miracles often accompanying the message.

As the founder of Outpouring Ministries (an organisation that exists to make a difference in a world full of desperate need), Steve has established mercy ministries in developing nations, constructing wells, computer and sewing schools, and establishing small to medium enterprises to permanently lift communities out of poverty.

He is also the founder of Global Influencers, a global community joined together in agape love and growing through the truth of God's Word and the fire of the Holy Spirit. Members are trained and equipped to walk in the fullness of the Gospel of the Kingdom, and to restore Kingdom culture from grassroots to government in the villages, cities, regions, and nations of the world.

Steve is commissioned through the Full Gospel Churches of Australia and ARC Global / H.I.M. He is the author of numerous books, and the composer of 3 worship CDs.

Worship CDs

www.globalinfluencers.org/resources
https://steveharris.hearnow.com
www.youtube.com/@steveharrisworship

Books

www.globalinfluencers.org/books

www.ingramcontent.com/pod-product-compliance
Lightning Source LLC
Chambersburg PA
CBHW032019290426
44109CB00013B/718